Beach
Wisdom

Life Lessons from the Ocean

By ELIZABETH COGSWELL BASKIN

Design and photography by KEITH BENNETT

Photography by TERRY ALLEN

**Andrews McMeel
Publishing, LLC**

Kansas City · Sydney · London

Andrews McMeel Publishing, LLC
an Andrews McMeel Universal company
1130 Walnut Street, Kansas City, Missouri 64106

www.andrewsmcmeel.com

12 13 14 15 16 WKT 16 15 14 13 12
ISBN: 978-0-7407-3310-9
Library of Congress Control Number: 2002111554

INTRODUCTION

This book is a reminder that some of the most useful spiritual lessons can be mastered with sand between our toes. Just what sort of wisdom, you might ask, can we pack up and take home with us from a trip to the beach?

The real answer is that the beach is a place where we rediscover our own wisdom. There we'll be, walking along on the sand, thinking about nothing much but the way the sun is sparkling on the water and that nice sandwich we'll have for lunch and trying to remember how long you're supposed to wait after you eat until it's safe to go in for a swim. And suddenly, whom should we bump into but our own highest selves, dishing out all kinds of wisdom we forgot we knew.

That's what the beach does. It gives us a chance to hear the truths our own hearts whisper and to slow our careening inner pace to something that more closely matches the ancient rhythms of the tides. When that happens, the answers we're looking for begin to float up to the surface. Grace begins to seep in, like the high tide slowly moving up the shore.

Faith also washes up. We watch the tide come in and the tide go out, just as it has for all the many generations before us. Perhaps the gift of the tides is to help us hold more faith in the ebb and flow of our own shifting fortunes or the rise and fall of our careers or even the waxing and waning of our loves.

The beach also reminds us of the playfulness of childhood and can even make us childlike again. I've seen serious, hardworking grown-ups, lawyers even, chortle like children as they dive under and bob over the waves. That streak of joy that resides within us is more apt to flash in the brilliant sunshine.

A trip to the beach has the power to restore us to ourselves, to even our keels, to lighten our hearts—at the very least, to put a little color in our cheeks.

Imagine yourself there, and already, as you picture that blue water stretching out to the horizon, you begin to hunch those shoulders a little less. You might begin to grasp your days less tightly, to let life flow more easily, like warm white sand sifting through your fingers, and maybe even to realize that many of things that make us wring our hands and gnash our teeth are not that important after all, in the grand scheme of things.

Does that dolphin leaping through the air seem worried about some client meeting or that tuition check or what her mother-in-law thinks? Nope. Because the dolphin knows better. That dolphin understands she doesn't need any other reason to be happy out there dancing in the waves, except that she's out there dancing in the waves.

This reminds me of one of my favorite lessons I ever took home from the beach. One time around sunset I happened upon six or eight old ladies, about shoulder deep in the water, just hanging around talking. The sound of their laughter carried far up the beach. I got the feeling they'd been there all afternoon.

This is what I learned about living from them: Those old ladies were not afraid to get their hair wet. They were not in any hurry to be anywhere else. And they had the good sense to be floating around out there together, now touching the bottom, now gliding lightly above on a passing wave, laughing their fool heads off.

Perhaps that's the most important wisdom we can take away from the beach. Life is to be enjoyed. Let's dive in.

Go in the water, even if it's cold.

Everyone gets to go outside and play.

Kick off your shoes
whenever you get the chance.

Love colors everything.

One man's work is another man's play.

Just when you think it's getting too deep, you'll find a sandbar.

When you catch a wave, ride it.

16

Eventually, the sun will come out
from behind the clouds.

The
shells
you
find
are
the
ones
meant
for
you.

Remain amazed.

Sunsets mean you don't need a watch.

Sometimes it's more fun to do nothing at all.

If you feed one seagull,
you'll soon have many seagulls.

To find the best shells,
        you have to walk slowly.

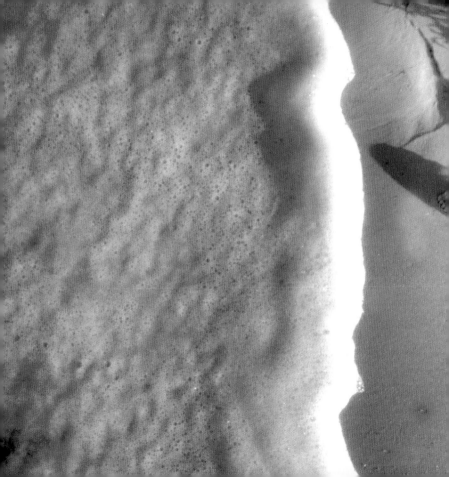

You'll find more perfect shells
than you can carry.

Who says you have to choose
between half empty and half full?

Sunsets happen every single day.

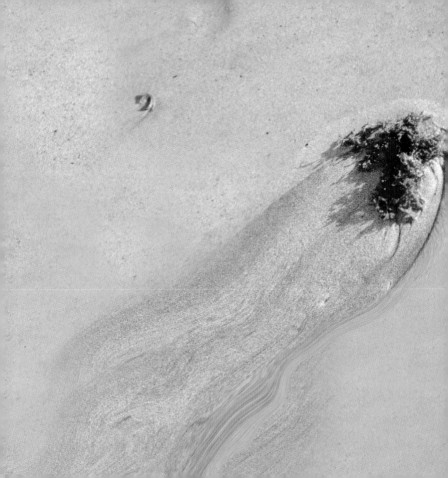

The tide comes in and the tide goes out.

Sand is part of the deal.

Rainy days also have their gifts.

Sand castles always get washed away.

The longer you look at the ocean
   the more you see.

There's great beauty even in rocky places.

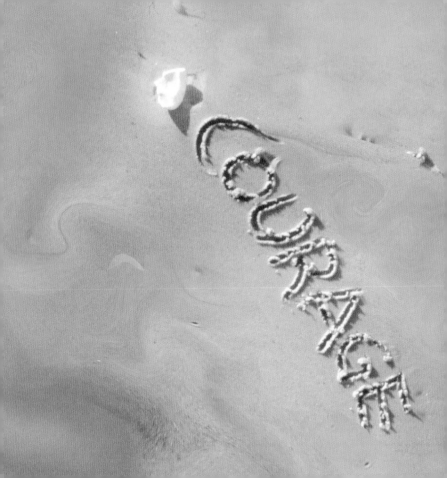

Fate loves a bold heart.

Sometimes the best thing is to jump right in.

Fear of sharks is generally exaggerated.

Sometimes there's no fighting the undertow.

Try not to shake your towel
upwind from other people.

Eventually it's time to go inside.